RICKMANSWORTH TO AYLESBURY

Vic Mitchell and Keith Smith

MP Middleton Press

Cover picture: Stoke Mandeville was woken from its Sunday afternoon slumber by the passage of the 10.10am Nottingham Victoria to Marylebone on 14th January 1962. It was hauled by class 5 4-6-0 no. 45116. (B.S.Jennings)

Published July 2005

ISBN 1 904474 61 6

© Middleton Press, 2005

Design Deborah Esher
Typesetting Emily Pede

Published by
        Middleton Press
        Easebourne Lane
        Midhurst, West Sussex
        GU29 9AZ
Tel: 01730 813169
Fax: 01730 812601
Email: info@middletonpress.co.uk
www.middletonpress.co.uk

Printed & bound by Biddles Ltd, Kings Lynn

INDEX

ACKNOWLEDGEMENTS

We are very grateful for the assistance received from many of those mentioned in the credits also to A.E.Bennett, R.S.Carpenter, G.Croughton, E.Hancock, M.A.N.Johnston, N.Langridge, Dr J.S.Manners, A.J.Reed, Mr D. and Dr S.Salter, M.J.Smith, D.Wilson, and particularly our ever supportive wives, Barbara Mitchell and Janet Smith.

I. Route map showing the early operators. (Railway Magazine)

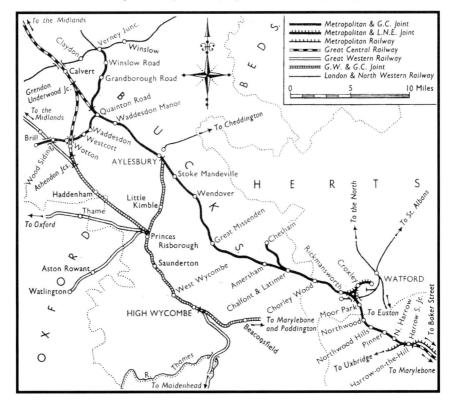

GEOGRAPHICAL SETTING

The market town of Rickmansworth is on the north side of the Colne Valley and at the foot of the dip slope of the Chiltern Hills, the Chalk of which is traversed for about 18 of the 21 miles of the route. The Chesham branch rises slightly from the main line and descends at mostly 1 in 60 into the upper part of the valley of the River Chess.

The route beyond Amersham drops onto the northern side of the valley of the River Misbourne, which rises near Great Missenden. North thereof, the line passes over the watershed and descends all the way to Aylesbury, running over outcrops of Upper Greensand and Gault Clay. This market town has Portland Beds and the headwaters of the River Thame in its vicinity.

The first three miles of the route is in the county of Hertfordshire and the remainder was built in Buckinghamshire.

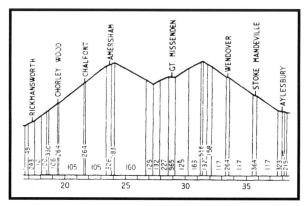

II. Gradient profile with mileage from Marylebone.

HISTORICAL BACKGROUND

Aylesbury received the first branch line in Britain and that was from the London and Birmingham Railway in 1839. It was for long operated by the London and North Western Railway.

The town's next branch was from Princes Risborough on the Wycombe Railway in 1863. The operator for over 80 years was the Great Western Railway. This company also worked the Aylesbury & Buckingham Railway's 1868 line to Verney Junction until 1891.

The Metropolitan Railway extended its operation out of London in stages and reached Rickmansworth on 1st September 1887. The next length opened was to Chesham on 8th July 1889 and the Chalfont & Latimer to Aylesbury section followed on 1st September 1892. The Great Central Railway began operating over the route on 15th March 1899, the services being between London and the Midlands. The section covered by this album came under the control of the Metropolitan & Great Central Joint Committee in 1906, the Act being in 1905.

The GCR became part of the London & North Eastern Railway in 1923, but the Joint Committee continued until nationalisation in 1948, administration alternating between the two companies every five years. Responsibility for civil engineering and signalling equipment was however divided permanently at mile-post 28½ (between Amersham and Great

Missenden), the GCR taking the north and the Metropolitan taking the south. This continued until nationalisation when the boundary was moved north to a point near Stoke Mandeville Hospital, just south of Aylesbury. It was repositioned to a location near milepost 25 at around the time that full electrification was extended from Rickmansworth to Amersham on 9th September 1961. There was some electric traction from 12th September 1960.

Upon nationalisation in 1948, the LNER became largely the Eastern Region of British Railways, but the former LNER-operated services within this volume were transferred to the London Midland Region on 1st February 1958. In 1987, they became part of the Thames & Chiltern area of Network SouthEast.

With the advent of privatisation, a franchise was let on 21st July 1996 to M40 Trains for Chiltern Railways to operate all services from Marylebone for seven years. Owing to its success, an extension to 2021 followed.

PASSENGER SERVICES

Down trains are described in this section. The initial service between Rickmansworth and Chesham provided one train per hour on weekdays and one every two hours on Sundays. After Chesham was served by branch line trains, there were two-hour intervals during the day and eight trains on Sundays, to that town. The Aylesbury route had a slightly smaller number of trains.

The 1905 Met timetable gave Chesham 24 weekday and 15 Sunday trains, Aylesbury receiving about half those numbers, but in addition there were 12 GCR trains from Marylebone on weekdays and four on Sundays. These dropped to eight and one respectively from April 1906, when many trains were transferred to the new route via High Wycombe. Prior to that, about one third of all GCR trains called at Rickmansworth and Great Missenden, but thereafter most ran fast to Aylesbury from London, Harrow or Northwood.

By 1925, Aylesbury was receiving a total of 26 trains on weekdays from the route, with 18 on Sundays. In 1943 the figures were 20 and 24. The 1959 timetable showed at least two trains in most hours daily. Of these, only four were long distance steam trains, these ceasing on 2nd March 1963.

The introduction of electric traction to Amersham brought a service improvement to that town, but only erratic DMUs north thereof subsequently. From 1974, they ran hourly from Marylebone on weekdays and from Amersham on Sundays. The few remaining trains to run north of Aylesbury were withdrawn on 4th September 1966.

NSE made a dramatic improvement in 1991 with the introduction of a basic 30-minute interval service between Marylebone and Aylesbury, although hourly on Sundays. London Transport have maintained a four per hour frequency to Amersham. The Chesham branch has had a shuttle service (except at peak times) operating half-hourly daily.

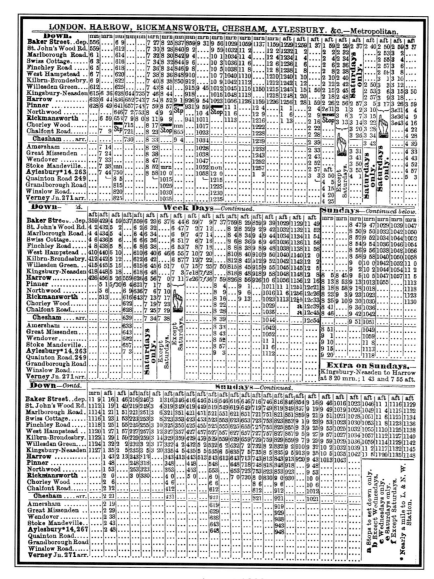

August 1893

Aylesbury - Chesham - Rickmansworth - Watford - London

All trains 🅐 except the 3 37 train from Woodford, on which first class is provided

No. 1. — MONDAY to FRIDAY—morning

WOODFORD & HINTON	3 37																							
Culworth																								
Helmdon																								
Brackley *Central*																								
Finmere																								
Calvert																								
Quainton Road																								
AYLESBURY ... arr.	A4 18																							
AYLESBURY ...dep.								6 7						6 36			6 52							
Stoke Mandeville								6 13						6 42			6 58							
Wendover								6 20						6 49			7 5							
Great Missenden								6 30						6 59			7 15							
Amersham								6 40						7 9			7 25							
CHESHAM ... arr.								6 56									7 50							
CHESHAM ...dep.				5 40				6 34					7 3			7 30			7 29					
Chalfont & Latimer				5 49				6 45					7 14			7 34			7 39					
Chorley Wood				5 53	J			6 49					7 18						7 43					
WATFORD			5 47			6 5	6 27		6 46		6 58	7 5		7 19		7 27	7 35		7 43					
Croxley Green			5 49			6 7	6 29		6 48		7 0	7 7		7 21		7 29	7 37		7 45					
Rickmansworth ... arr.				5 58					6 54					7 23			7 39		7 48					
Rickmansworth ...dep.		5 37		5 59		6 20		6 40		6 58			7 15		7 27		7 43		7 52					
Moor Park & Sandy Lodge							6 34	6 44	6 53	7 2	7 5	7 12	7 19		7 26	7 31	7 34	7 42	7 47	7 50	7 56			
Northwood		5 43	5 56	6 6	6 14	6 26	6 37	6 47	6 56		7 8	7 15	7 22		7 29		7 37	7 45		7 53				
Northwood Hills		5 46	5 59	6 9	6 17	6 29	6 40	6 50	6 59		7 11	7 18	7 25		7 32		7 40	7 48		7 56				
Pinner		5 49	6 2	6 13	6 20	6 32	6 43	6 53	7 2		7 14	7 21	7 28		7 35		7 43	7 51		7 59				
North Harrow		5 52	6 5	6 16	6 23	6 35	6 46	6 56	7 5		7 17	7 24	7 31		7 38		7 46	7 54		8 2				
HARROW on the Hill		5 56	6 9	6 21	6 27	6 38	6 49	7 1	7 10		7 23	7 29	7 36		7 43		7 50	7 59		8 7				
Northwick Park		5 58	6 11		6 29	6 40	6 51	7 3	7 12		7 25	7 31			7 45			8 1		8 9				
Preston Road		6 1	6 14		6 32	6 43	6 54	7 6	7 16		7 28	7 34			7 49			8 4		8 13				
Wembley Park		6 3	6 17		6 34	6 45	6 56	7 9	7 18		7 30	7 36	7 41		7 51		7 56	8 6		8 15				
Finchley Road		6 11	6 26		6 44	6 54	7 4	7 17	7 27	7 24	7 38	7 44	7 50		7 59	7 57	8 5	8 15	8 12	8 24	8 21			
BAKER STREET		6 16	6 31		6 49	6 59	7 9	7 22	7 32	7 29	7 43	7 49	7 55		8 4	8 2	8 10	8 20	8 17	8 29	8 26			
MARYLEBONE	5 15			6 36																				
Kings Cross St. Pancras			6 38				7 16	7 32	7 40	7 36		7 56	8 2		8 10	8 17	8 28	8 25	8 36					
Moorgate			6 44				7 22	7 38	7 46	7 42		8 2	8 8		8 16	8 23	8 34	8 31	8 42					
Liverpool Street			6 46				7 24	7 40	7 48	7 44		8 4	8 10		8 18	8 25	8 36	8 33	8 44					
ALDGATE			6 48				7 26	7 42	7 50			8 6	8 12			8 27	8 38							

June 1947

Aylesbury - Chesham - Rickmansworth - Watford - London

All trains 🅐 except the 6 45 train from Brackley *Central* and the 7 38 train from Woodford, on which first class is provided

No. 2. — MONDAY to FRIDAY—morning

WOODFORD & HINTON																7 38						
Culworth																7 45						
Helmdon																7 53						
Brackley *Central*						6 45										8 1						
Finmere						6 54										8 10						
Calvert						7 4										8 20						
Quainton Road						7 12										8 28						
AYLESBURY ... arr.						7 21										8 37						
AYLESBURY ...dep.		7 12			7 26				7 48		8 4			8 20		8 42						
Stoke Mandeville		7 18			7 32				7 54		8 10			8 26		8 48						
Wendover		7 25			7 39	7 50			8 2		8 17			8 33		8 55						
Great Missenden		7 35			7 49				8 13		8 27			8 43		9 5		9 13				
Amersham		7 45			8 0	8 7			8 25		8 37			8 53		9 15		9 23				
CHESHAM ... arr.					8 29	8 29								9 10				9 37				
CHESHAM ...dep.					7 54			8 9			8 31		8 42		8 47			9 16				
Chalfont & Latimer		7 50			8 5		8 12	8 19			8 35		8 46		8 58			9 28				
Chorley Wood		7 54					8 16	8 23							9 2			9 32				
WATFORD	7 52		8 3				8 15	8 23	8 33		8 44		8 54			9 11		9 24		9 38		
Croxley Green	7 54		8 5				8 17	8 25	8 35		8 46		8 56			9 13		9 26		9 40		
Rickmansworth ... arr.		7 59			8 13		8 21		8 40				8 51		9 7			9 37				
Rickmansworth ...dep.			8 3	8 10	8 15		8 22		8 32	8 41		8 54		9 2	9 10			9 38				
Moor Park & Sandy Lodge	7 59	8 3	8 7					8 30	8 36	8 40	8 45	8 51	8 58	9 1	9 6	9 14		9 31	9 42	9 45		
Northwood	8 2			8 13	8 17	8 22	8 25	8 29	8 33	8 43		8 54		9 4	9 9		9 21		9 34	9 48		
Northwood Hills	8 5			8 16	8 20		8 28	8 32	8 36	8 46		8 56		9 6	9 11		9 23		9 37	9 50		
Pinner	8 8			8 19	8 23	8 27	8 31		8 39	8 49		8 59		9 9	9 14		9 26		9 40	9 53		
North Harrow	8 11			8 22	8 26		8 34	8 38	8 42	8 52		9 2		9 12	9 17		9 29		9 43	9 56		
HARROW on the Hill	8 15			8 26	8 30	8 34	8 39	8 43	8 46	8 57	9 1	9 6		9 16	9 21		9 32	9 54	9 46	9 59		
Northwick Park					8 32					8 59					9 23		9 34		9 48	10 1		
Preston Road					8 36					9 2					9 27		9 37		9 51	10 4		
Wembley Park	8 20		8 31	8 38		8 45		8 52		9 4		9 11		9 22	9 29		9 39		9 53	10 6		
Finchley Road	8 28	8 31	8 40	8 47		8 54		9 1	9 3	9 13		9 20	9 23	9 30	9 38	9 35	9 47		10 2	10 14		
BAKER STREET	8 33	8 36	8 45	8 52		8 59		9 6	9 9	9 18		9 25	9 28	9 35	9 43	9 40	9 52		10 7	10 19		
MARYLEBONE					8 49		8 58				9 18					9 49		10 11				
Kings Cross St. Pancras		8 44			8 59		9 6		9 13	9 17	9 25		9 32	9 36		9 48	10 0		10 14			
Moorgate		8 50			9 5		9 12		9 19	9 23	9 31		9 38	9 42	9 50		9 54	10 6		10 20		
Liverpool Street		8 52			9 7		9 14		9 21	9 25			9 40	9 44	9 52		9 56	10 8		10 22		
ALDGATE					9 9		9 16		9 23				9 42		9 54			10 10				

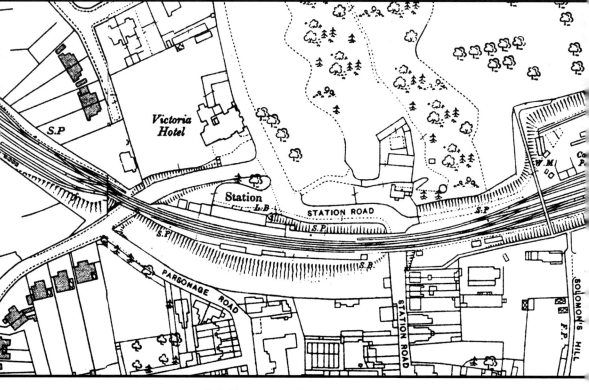

RICKMANSWORTH

III.   The 1937 edition shows the goods yard at its optimum. The local gasworks was in Wharf Lane and probably received most of its coal by canal in its early years; gas was supplied from Watford after 1920. The upper two tracks on the left are electrified carriage sidings and the upper one on the right is the goods yard headshunt.

1.   Smoke obscures the signal box as Met A class 4-4-0T no.45 arrives from London around the turn of the century. The badly placed water column was moved later. There was a 25 mph speed limit on the curves here. (Lens of Sutton coll.)

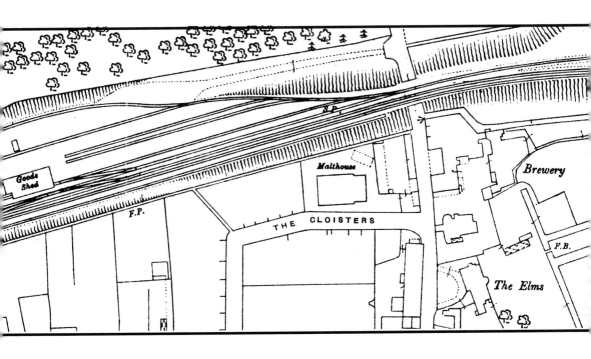

2.   The column was some distance from the end of the up platform, as were the signals. These operational inconveniences have not been explained. After electrification, some EMUs terminated at this platform and then continued to the berthing sidings beyond. (Lens of Sutton coll.)

3.   From 1925 to 1961, the locomotives of Aylesbury trains were changed here. On the left of the map are the two short sidings added for this purpose. No.14 *Benjamin Disraeli* has arrived from London on 17th August 1935 and is returning eastwards, as class H 4-4-4T no. 106 backs towards its train. (H.C.Casserley)

4.   At the other end of the station on 27th April 1946, class E 0-4-4T no. L.48 waits in the bay platform on standby duties, as LNER 2-6-4T no. 6160 arrives with a train for Baker Street. The engine was formerly Met no. 113 and will soon be detached in favour of an electric locomotive. (H.C.Casserley)

5.   The 3.30pm Marylebone to Manchester was hauled by class V2 2-6-2 no. 983 on 10th September 1946. Its first stop was at Aylesbury at 4.36, although it called at Harrow "to take up only." (H.C.Casserley)

6.   LT 0-4-4T no. L.44 has just been coupled to the 3.45pm from Baker Street to Aylesbury, due to the non-availability of the scheduled BR locomotive on 12th August 1951. Formerly Metropolitan no. 1, this engine was preserved and usually resides at the Buckinghamshire Railway Centre. (N.W.Sprinks)

7.   An ex-LMS class 4 2-6-4T arrives on 9th September 1960 with an Aylesbury to Baker Street service. It will soon be replaced by an electric locomotive, the boards on the sleepers facilitating the operation. (T.Wright)

8.   One of the replacement class 115 DMUs was recorded from the same point on 28th July 1990. Opened on 25th July 1955, the signal box is seen more clearly; the roofing had been replaced in 1985, when the platforms were rebuilt due to subsidence. (S.P.Derek)

9.	During the "Steam on the Met" event of 1996, preserved ex-GWR Mogul no. 7325 heads an Amersham to Watford service through Rickmansworth on 19th May. This locomotive was normally at home on the Severn Valley Railway. (M.Turvey)

10.	"Steam on the Met" was a popular annual event and this photograph is from 16th May 1998. Ex-LMS 2-6-0 no. 2968 is passing the two berthing sidings seen behind no.14 in picture no.3. This loco was also based on the SVR. (D.Trevor Rowe)

Views of the other areas of the station can be found in the companion album, *Marylebone to Rickmansworth.*

11.	The exterior was showing LT and BR signs in October 2004, although the latter was intended to indicate a national railway station by that time. Note that the water tank was still in place. The ornate canopy brackets were initially replicated on the platforms - see picture 6. (V.Mitchell)

CHORLEYWOOD

Chorleywood Kennels

Union & U.D.Bdy.

3ft.R.H.

B.H.

L.B.

Misn. Hall

C

IV.   The 1914 survey reveals the limited residential development at that time. The population rose from 1180 in 1901 to 7100 in 1961. The lowest track was a headshunt.

Chorleywood Hotel

S.P.

S.P.

S.P.

Station

S.P.

S.B.

Old Gravel Pit

L O W E R   R O A D

S.P.

NORTH ROAD

12.   Southbound on 2nd June 1934 is Met K class 2-6-4T no. 111, which became LNER class L2 no. 6158. The line carried few through freight trains, as the High Wycombe route was more easily graded. (H.C.Casserley)

13.   No. 69842 was one of the GCR class A5s built by the LNER for its NE area. It was one of five allocated to Neasden and was hauling the 5.21pm Aylesbury to Baker Street on 28th June 1951, a Met service. Note the wood grain on the coach panels. (N.W.Sprinks)

14.   Also running on the same day was ex-LNER class N7 0-6-2T no. 69692. It was working the Met's 5.36pm Liverpool Street to Chesham service. This was usually hauled by a class C13 4-4-2T at that time. (N.W.Sprinks)

15.   Met T stock appeared on the route only from September 1960 until October 1962 and, had all the A60 stock been delivered on time, would have never done so. This view is from August 1961. (T.Wright)

16.   DMUs first appeared on the route regularly in the Autumn of 1961, with one evening rush hour working. The goods yard closed on 14th November 1966; the photo was taken ten weeks before. (T.Wright)

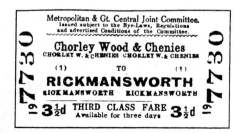

17.   The suffix "and Chenies" was used from 1915 to 1934. This and the next picture are from July 1987. The Metropolitan Railway Country Estates Company created extensive luxury housing in this area. (D.Thompson)

18.   Standard Met architectural plans were employed, as was the usual yellow brick. Chorley Wood became one word in railway use in 1965. Local first class travel ceased in 1941. (D.Thompson)

19.   The first appearance of a class 115 DMU on the line was on a trial run in January 1961. This example was recorded working the 13.39 from Aylesbury on 28th July 1990. The signal box had closed in 1955. (S.P.Derek)

20. The "Steam on the Met" event included GWR 0-6-0PT no.9466 piloted by Met 0-4-4T no. 1 on 29th July 1990. The arch once carried cables over the sidings and appears in the background of picture 16. (M.Turvey)

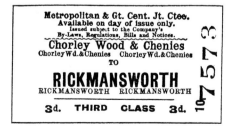

Metropolitan & Gt. Cent. Jt. Ctee.
Available on day of issue only.
Issued subject to the Company's
By-Laws, Regulations, Bills and Notices.
Chorley Wood & Chenies
Chorley Wd.&Chenies   Chorley Wd.&Chenies
TO
RICKMANSWORTH
RICKMANSWORTH   RICKMANSWORTH
3d.   THIRD   CLASS   3d.

10 7573

3rd Cl   M&GC
Issued subject to the Bye-Laws Regulations
and Conditions of the Committee.
Available for three Days.
CHORLEY WOOD to
Chorley Wood   Chorley Wood
RICKMANSWORTH (M&GC)
CHALFONT & LATIMER
6d   6d

-8460   8460

21.   Bound for Marylebone on 27th May 2000 is no. 165008. DMUs of this type provided two of the six departures each hour in the basic weekday timetable at that time. (M.Turvey)

CHALFONT & LATIMER

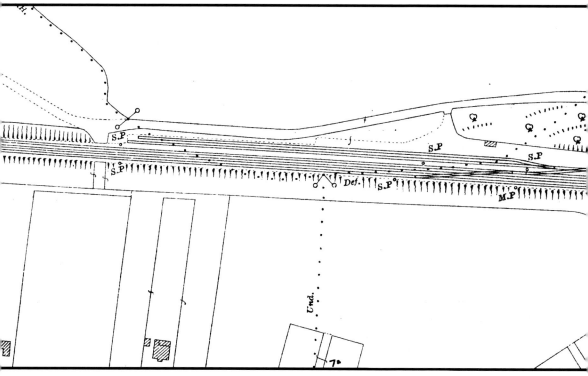

V.   The 1925 edition has the single line to Chesham on the left, at the top.

22.   The connection to the branch is opposite the signal box on the left. The loco of the mixed train is nearby. The photo is from about 1905, when the long signal arms were still in use. (Lens of Sutton coll.)

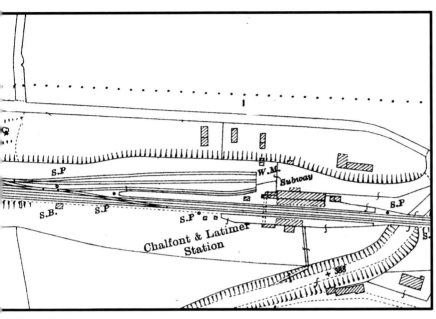

23.   An up GCR train approaches at around the same period, with three horse boxes in the formation. Near the branch locomotive is an animal feedstuff mill and in its train is a light panelled first class coach. (Lens of Sutton coll.)

→

24.   Few railways operated 4-4-4Ts, but no. 109 was one of a successful batch on the Met. It is bound for Rickmansworth on 21st May 1934, but its train will go on to London.
(H.F.Wheeller/R.S.Carpenter coll.)

25.   Recorded on the same day is 0-4-4T no. 77 with a train from Chesham. The original signal arms had been modified, but the post caps remained unaltered.
(H.F.Wheeller/R.S.Carpenter coll.)

→

26.   Both platforms received canopy extensions, probably in the late 1930s. The sign proclaims plain "Chalfont" and beyond it is a push-pull unit. (Lens of Sutton coll.)

27.   Class E 0-4-4T no. L.44 was standby loco at Rickmansworth on 12th August 1951 when an up express engine from Manchester failed. The class L1 2-6-4T that was due to go to Aylesbury replaced it and L.44 took the lighter train north. (J.H.Meredith)

28.   The reverse curves of the bay track are evident on 9th September 1951. Ex-GCR class C13 4-4-2T no. 67418 waits with ex-Met coaches, which had been converted to electric operation and then back to steam. (N.W.Sprinks)

29.   This westward view is from 1957, when the signs proclaimed the full name. It was Chalfont Road until 1st November 1915. (B.W.Leslie/GCR Society)

30.   This train-less view from 1957 has the merit of showing the curvature at the end of the bay platform clearly. The junction signal is right of centre. (D.B.Clayton)

31.   Working the branch on 15th March 1959 was LMS-designed and BR-built 2-6-2T no. 41284. It is arriving with the 4.43pm from Chesham. (B.W.Leslie/GCR Society)

32.   Part of the goods yard is evident, this closing on 14th November 1966. Heading north on 19th August 1960 is class B1 4-6-0 no. 61368, while steam issues from below the driving compartment of the branch shuttle. (T.Wright)

33.   The simple north elevation was recorded in July 1987. The curved canopy of the bay is on the right. (D.Thompson)

34.   To add variety to the "Steam on the Met" on 29th July 1990, and to give air braking, LT provided a battery locomotive on the rear of the 13.10 Harrow to Amersham. On the left are the speed limits for the two routes in that vicinity. (P.G.Barnes)

35.   The junction was recorded on 27th May 2000 as an EMU arrives from Chesham and a DMU approaches in the distance. Only a few peak hour trains on Mondays - Fridays used the junction. (M.Turvey)

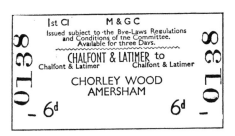

Chesham Branch

36. The branch single line (right) runs parallel to the main lines for almost one mile. Formerly Met class F, 0-6-2T no. L.49 is working an engineers train during a possession on 28th October 1951. (N.W.Sprinks)

37. Running on the branch on 10th May 1952 is ex-GCR class C13 4-4-2T no.67420 with the 1.34pm Liverpool Street to Chesham, a Saturdays-only working in the days of the 5½ day week. Flat bottom rail is now in place on the up track. (N.W.Sprinks)

38. Sister locomotive no. 67418 veers away from the main line on Christmas Day 1953 and gives us a fine view of the historic "Chesham Set" as it propels the coaches towards the Chess Valley. They were introduced to the branch in 1941 and are now preserved on the Bluebell Railway. (N.W.Sprinks)

39.   With the conductor rails already in place, a class 4 2-6-4T descends the multi-curved 1 in 60 gradient to Chesham on 19th August 1960. It is a through train from Baker Street. (T.Wright)

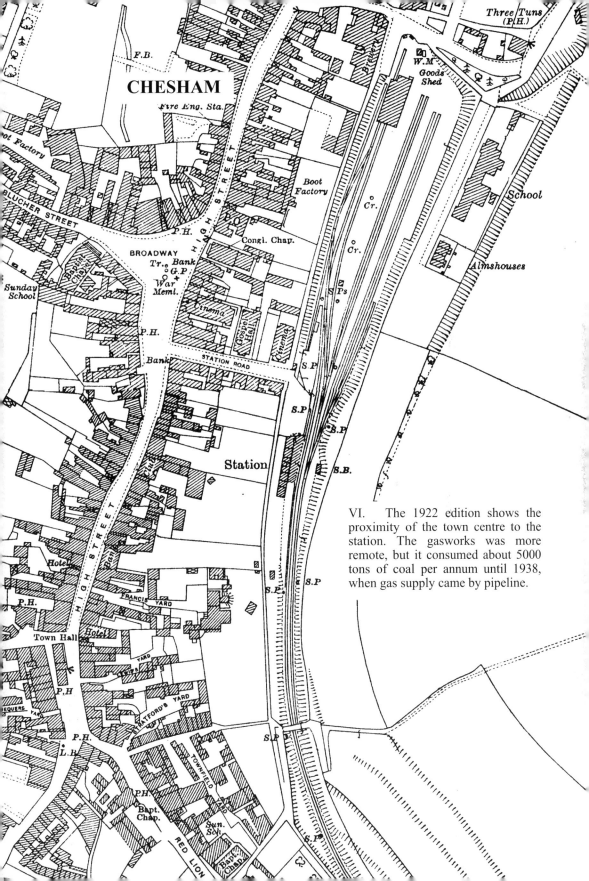

CHESHAM

Three Tuns (P.H.)

F.B.

Fire Eng. Sta.

W.M Goods Shed

Boot Factory

BLUCHER STREET

P.H.

Cr.

School

BROADWAY

Congl. Chap.

Tr. Bank
G.P.
War Meml.

Cr.

Sunday School

Bapt. Chapel

Cinema

S.Ps

Almshouses

P.H.

Gospel Hall

Cinema

Bank

STATION ROAD

S.P.

S.P.

S.P.

Station

S.B.

S.B.

HIGH STREET

VI.   The 1922 edition shows the proximity of the town centre to the station. The gasworks was more remote, but it consumed about 5000 tons of coal per annum until 1938, when gas supply came by pipeline.

Hotel

FRANCIS YARD

Hotel

S.P.

S.P

P.H.

Town Hall

P.H

STRATFORD'S YARD

CHEQUERS YARD

P.H.

L.B.

P.H.

TOWNFIELD

Bapt. Chap.

Sun. Sch.

S.P.

RED LION

Bapt Chapel

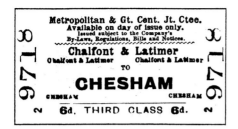

40.   This northward view is thought to have been recorded soon after the opening in 1889. The signals are for goods trains and empty stock. (Lens of Sutton coll.)

41.   The driver of Met 0-4-4T no. 79 has received the electric tablet for the single line, sometime in the 1930s. Track circuiting and co-acting automatically locked signals were installed in 1949. (Lens of Sutton coll.)

42.   A full Sunday service was operated on Christmas Day 1953 by no. 67418. There is evidence of steam heating of the train, but one doubts if many benefited from it. Such service did not last much longer nationally. (N.W.Sprinks)

43.   The rural setting of the station is evident in this 1957 panorama. Even today, the terminus is on the eastern flank of the town. Pronunciation locally is often "Chess'm" or "Chezem". (D.B.Clayton)

44. The jib of the crane is visible; it could cope with a load of eight tons. Beyond it is the goods shed; traffic ceased on 4th July 1966 and the yard gradually became a car park. The brewery chimney is in the background. (D.B.Clayton)

45. Goods inward included much timber for furniture and brush manufacture; look back at picture 22 for evidence. Domestic coal was an important part of the business, but this declined after 1960, the year of this photograph. (Milepost 92½)

46.   The north elevation was recorded in 1959. Upon entering, the booking office was on the right and the waiting room was beyond that, but it is not now the case. (J.C.Gillham)

47.   The end was nigh for steam as class 2 2-6-2T no. 41272 departs with the Ashbury-built coaches on 9th September 1960. The track on the left was newly laid. (T.Wright)

48.   The last day of steam on the branch on 11th September 1960 generated much emotion and a wreath for no. 41284. Vast crowds gathered later that day. (Milepost 92½)

49.   The classic Met box had the diagonal boarding much loved in the Victorian period. The box was retained after closure on 29th November 1960, as it contained much essential equipment. (Lens of Sutton coll.)

50.   For only a short period from August 1960 were the peak-hour London trains electrically hauled. No. 16 is running round on the last day of operation, 9th September 1961. These locomotives were withdrawn from regular service that day. The signals are in transition - colour light on the platform and semaphore for the loop. (Colour Rail)

51.   DMUs replaced steam on the 03.55 newspaper train from Marylebone in 1960. The station lights glow as the return working is about to depart at 05.58 in July 1962. This service ceased on 17th October 1967, after which time the branch was Met operated exclusively. (Colour Rail)

52.   The last T stock was operated by LT on 5th October 1962. An A60 unit was photographed on 18th April 2005, when the signal box was still standing. The bay platform was closed in 1973 and the station was extensively refurbished in 1992-93, winning an award. (V.Mitchell)

AMERSHAM

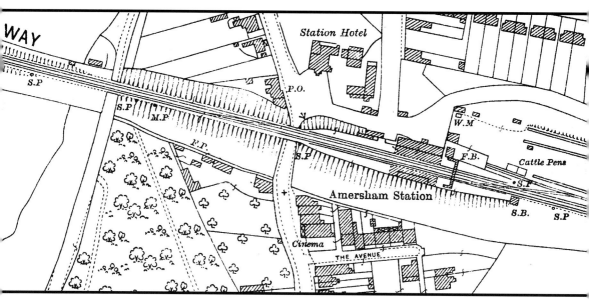

VII. The 1925 survey shows limited development near the station; the old town was down in the valley and had only 2674 inhabitants in 1901. Growth took place near the station and the figure reached 18,310 for the 1961 census.

53. This view towards Aylesbury is probably from the 1930s and has the signal box to the left of the camera, convenient for control of the crossover, which also had a connection to the goods yard. (Lens of Sutton coll.)

(lower right) 54. This fine panorama of the goods yard on 7th July 1956 shows still little development in the area. Class 4 2-6-0 no. 76039 is leaving the yard by the eastern connection. Goods traffic ceased on 4th July 1966. (B.W.Leslie/GCR Society)

1632

Metropolitan Railway
NOT TRANSFERABLE
Available on day of issue only.
AMERSHAM
Series 1) AMERSHAM   AMERSHAM (L
TO
CHORLEY WOOD
CHORLEY WOOD   CHORLEY WOOD
FARE 4d THIRD CLASS 4d

1632

225

Metropolitan & Gt. Cent. Jt. Ctee.
Available on day of issue only.
Issued subject to the Company's
By-Laws, Regulations, Bills and Notices.
Amersham
Amersham   Amersham
TO
CHORLEY WOOD&CHENIES
Chorley W.&Chenies   Chorley W.&Chenies
— 7d. THIRD CLASS 7d. —

225

Goods Shed

S.P

55.   A view from the same footbridge on 20th September 1958 features class L1 2-6-4T no. 67743 with the 2.52pm (Saturdays only) Brackley to Marylebone service. The down refuge siding was a late addition. (B.W.Leslie/GCR Society)

56.   The signal box is evident as 2-6-4T no. 42249 comes to a stand with the 12.15pm Baker Street to Aylesbury service on 23rd March 1958. (B.W.Leslie/GCR Society)

57.   The suffix "& Chesham Bois" was in use from 1922 until 1934 officially, although the signs remained until 1948. This 1958 view towards London includes the goods shed. The down platform would soon become an island. (B.W Leslie/GCR Society)

58.   The exterior was recorded on 20th September 1959; little had changed since its construction, but a street of modern shops had developed opposite the entrance. (J.C.Gillham)

60.   The 10.38 departure for Baker Street was formed of A60 stock on 9th September 1969. A second footbridge is seen, this spanning three electrified tracks and the goods loop. (B.W.Leslie)

59.   As seen elsewhere, the oldest trains were used over the newest electric rails for a short period initially. T stock was recorded at the up platform on 3rd September 1961. Electrification brought 20 extra trains on each weekday. (J.C.Gillham)

61.   The bridge on the right of the map is the viewpoint for this picture, also nos 54 and 55. A DMU from Aylesbury is about to use the crossover in the foreground, in order to return there on 29th July 1990. In the siding are the locos seen in picture 20. (P.G.Barnes)

62.   Ex-LNER 0-6-2T no.69621 from the East Anglia Railway Museum runs in on 23rd May 1992, carrying the Amersham Centenary headboard. The multi-storey car park in the background is on the site of the goods yard; it is under construction in the previous picture. (M.Turvey)

63.   To deal with any fires that day, each of the steam specials between Amersham and Harrow-on-the-Hill and reverse was followed by a Metropolitan Line electric train containing a team of fire fighters. The train is seen heading out of Amersham following the 12.40 service to Harrow. No. 69621 is standing in the centre platform. (M.Turvey)

64.   Trains bound for Aylesbury use the 1961 southern platform, as seen on 24th September 1997. The 1961 long footbridge had to be replaced in 1989; it spans the space once occupied by the goods loop. (F.Hornby)

WEST OF AMERSHAM

65.   Two electrified sidings were provided west of the station in 1961 for terminating LT trains. An A60 EMU is doing so on 26th May 1963, as an up DMU passes on its left. One of the 20 electric locos built for the Met, no. 5 *John Hampden,* stands in the other siding having just arrived with the Centenary special. (J.C.Gillham)

⟶

66.   Two miles from the station, a footpath crosses the line to run behind Mantles Farm. No. 42133 speeds east with the 3.50pm Aylesbury to Liverpool Street on 1st September 1961. A signal box called "Mantles Wood" was built in this vicinity in 1900. (L.W.Rowe)

67.   A York based loco appeared on 11th April 1953 in the form of ex-NER class B16/3 no. 61463. It is hauling the 1.03pm Brackley to Marylebone stopping train and is climbing at 1 in 160. (N.W.Sprinks)

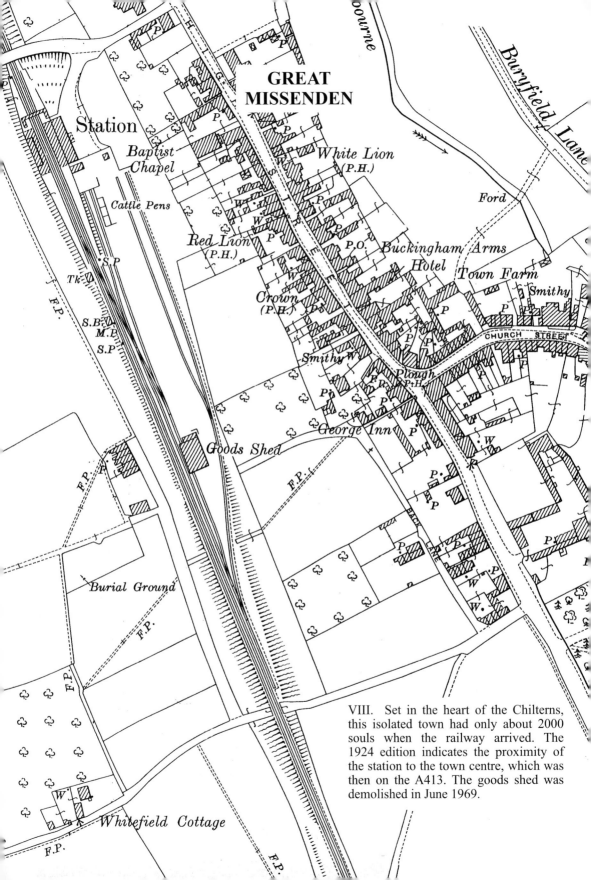

GREAT
MISSENDEN

Station

Baptist
Chapel

Cattle Pens

White Lion
(P.H.)

Ford

Red Lion
(P.H.)

P.O.

Buckingham Arms
Hotel

Town Farm

Smithy

·S.P.

Tk·D

Crown
(P.H.)

CHURCH   STREET

S.B.
M.P.
S.P.

Smithy W

Plough
(P.H.)

F.P.

Goods Shed

F.P.

George Inn

W

F.P.

Burial Ground

F.P.

W

W

VIII. Set in the heart of the Chilterns,
this isolated town had only about 2000
souls when the railway arrived. The
1924 edition indicates the proximity of
the station to the town centre, which was
then on the A413. The goods shed was
demolished in June 1969.

Whitefield Cottage

F.P.

F.P.

Burryfield Lane

68. An eastward postcard view from the road bridge for the lane to Prestwood features a horse box, a milk van and a parcels van, which typify early local traffic. (Lens of Sutton coll.)

69. Curious lettering was used on this boundary post, which was photographed in 1951, by which time the boundary was near Aylesbury. It was ½ mile to the south of the station. (N.W.Sprinks)

70.   The cattle pens are evident as are the points to the refuge siding in the foreground. The
signal box had 30 levers. The ex-LSWR class T9 4-4-0 was no. 30719 and it appeared on 15th
May 1955 with the "William Penn Special," a ramblers excursion from Waterloo.
(Lens of Sutton coll.)

1157

Metropolitan & Gt. Central Joint Committee.
Issued subject to the Bye-Laws, Regulations
and advertised Conditions of the Committee.

Great Missenden

Great Missenden   Great Missenden
1)   TO   (1

WEMBLEY PARK

WEMBLEY PARK   WEMBLEY PARK
Via Harrow

— 2/10 THIRD CLASS FARE 2/10 —
Available day of issue only.

1157

71.   Bound for Rickmansworth, class 4 2-6-4T no. 42252 runs in with an Aylesbury - Baker Street train at 4.28pm on 9th September 1960. (T.Wright)

72.   The canopies were still complete on 1st September 1962 when ex-LMS "Jubilee" class 4-6-0 no. 45556 *Nova Scotia* sped through with the 8.45am Nottingham Victoria to Marylebone. (B.S.Jennings)

73.　　When photographed on 9th June 1979, the down platform had only a small shelter, usually sufficient for the small number of passengers departing in that direction. The demolition took place in 1964. (B.W Leslie)

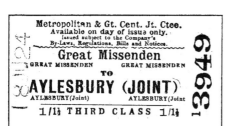

Metropolitan & Gt. Cent. Jt. Ctee.
Available on day of issue only.
Issued subject to the Company's
By-Laws, Regulations, Bills and Notices.
Great Missenden
GREAT MISSENDEN　　GREAT MISSENDEN
TO
AYLESBURY (JOINT)
AYLESBURY (Joint)　　AYLESBURY (Joint)
1/1½ THIRD CLASS 1/1½
13949

3rd Cl　　M & GC　　1
Issued subject to the Bye-Laws Regulations
and Conditions of the Committee.
Available for three Days.
GREAT MISSENDEN to
Great Missenden　　Great Missenden
AMERSHAM
AMERSHAM　　AMERSHAM
R 10d　　R 10d
3290

74.	The prospective passenger's perspective was recorded in August 1983, little changing in the previous or the subsequent decades. The station was much used by hikers from London between the wars. (B.W.Leslie)

75.	We can enjoy another peaceful scene from 1983, a far cry from 1907 when a 1.40pm express from Marylebone was introduced, which shed a slip coach at Amersham at 2.13, Saturdays only. This terminated here at 2.24, as did the 8.12am train from London which called only at Rickmansworth. (B.W.Leslie)

76.   Interior modernisation and valence repairs explain the debris on 11th November 1989. After an initial dip, the line climbs at 1 in 125 for over one mile into the distance. (P.G.Barnes)

77.   Looking south on the same day, we note that semaphore signals were still in use. The site on the left had been occupied by the goods yard until 4th July 1966. The box had 30 levers. (P.G.Barnes)

June 1951

THE MASTER CUTLER
Restaurant Car Express
SHEFFIELD, NOTTINGHAM, LEICESTER, RUGBY, LONDON (Marylebone)

WEEKDAYS

	a.m.		p.m.
Sheffield (Victoria) ... dep	7 40	London (Marylebone) dep	6 15
Nottingham (Victoria) ,,	8 43	Rugby (Central) ... ... arr	8 6
Leicester (Central) ... ,,	9A18	Leicester (Central) ... ,,	8 31
Rugby (Central) ... ... ,,	9A46	Nottingham (Victoria) ,,	9 4
London (Marylebone)... arr	11A25	Sheffield (Victoria) ... ,,	10 11

A—On Saturdays departs Leicester (Central) 9 22, Rugby (Central) 9 52, and arrives London (Marylebone) 11 35 a.m.

THE SOUTH YORKSHIREMAN

BRADFORD, HUDDERSFIELD, SHEFFIELD, NOTTINGHAM, LEICESTER, LONDON (Marylebone)

WEEKDAYS

	a.m.		p.m.
Bradford (Exchange) ...dep	10 0	London (Marylebone) dep	4 50
Huddersfield ... ... ,,	10 35	Aylesbury ... ... ,,	5 49
Sheffield (Victoria) ... ,,	11 27		
	p.m.	Leicester (Central) ...arr	7 0
Nottingham (Victoria) ,,	12 30	Nottingham (Victoria) ,,	7 33
Loughborough (Central) ,,	12 52	Sheffield (Victoria) ... ,,	8 35
Leicester (Central) ... ,,	1 11	Penistone ... ... ,,	9 3
Rugby (Central) ... ... ,,	1 39	Huddersfield ... ... ,,	9 28
Aylesbury ... ... arr	2 29	Bradford (Exchange) ... ,,	10 10
London (Marylebone)... ,,	3 29		

Restaurant Cars available between Sheffield (Victoria) and London (Marylebone).

Passengers travelling from Bradford (Exchange), Huddersfield, Sheffield (Victoria) and London (Marylebone) by these services can reserve seats in advance on payment of a fee of 1s. 0d. per seat.

SOUTH OF WENDOVER

78. The climb south was mostly at 1 in 117 and the summit was a little over 500ft above sea level, two miles south of the station. Class A3 4-6-2 no. 60051 *Blink Bonny* was barking loudly with the nine coaches of the 10.25am Manchester to Marylebone on 11th April 1952. (N.W.Sprinks)

79. The 3.08 Aylesbury to Liverpool Street was well illuminated on 1st September 1961, as it hurried south behind ex LMS 2-6-4T no. 42134. There was an intermediate signal box near Dutchlands Farm from 1900. (L.W.Rowe)

(lower right) 80. Great Missenden's up distant signal is evident as the 9.10am from Marylebone roars north, issuing steam in an embarrassing manner. Lower left is the fogmans hut, site of a lonely and dreary task. (P.G.Barnes)

WENDOVER

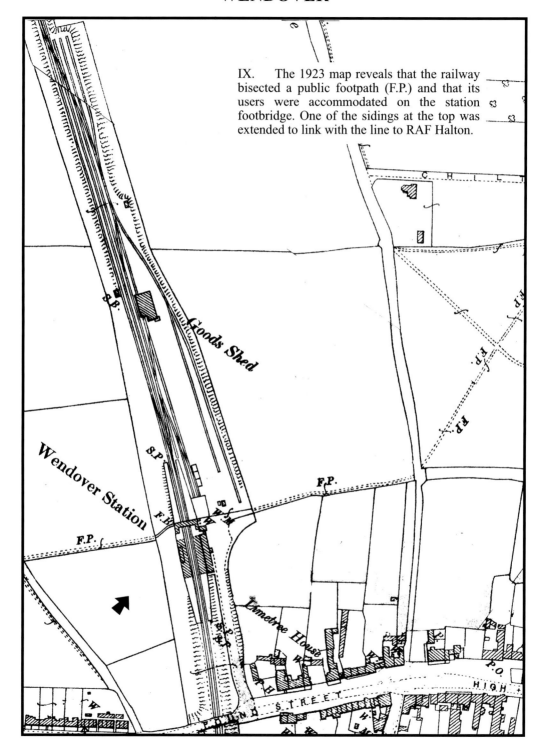

IX.   The 1923 map reveals that the railway bisected a public footpath (F.P.) and that its users were accommodated on the station footbridge. One of the sidings at the top was extended to link with the line to RAF Halton.

81.   This postcard appears to depict a GCR class 9K 4-4-2T departing for London in about 1920. The station is on the western flank of the town, the population of which rose from 2009 in 1901 to 6151 in 1961. The Met publicity described it as "The Pearl of the Chilterns." (Lens of Sutton coll.)

82.   The Royal Train and Princess Mary visited the station probably when the latter was travelling to Halton House. No. 1038 was one of a batch of 4-4-0s built by Sharp Stewart in 1903 for the GCR and classified 11B. They became LNER class D9. (P.M.Cowan coll.)

83.   This postcard panorama of the busy goods yard was created from the bridge seen in picture 81 and seems to include the same type of loco. It is blowing off after climbing at 1 in 117 for almost two miles. (Lens of Sutton coll.)

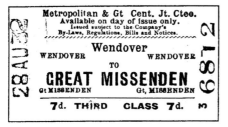

Metropolitan & Gt Cent. Jt. Ctee.
Available on day of issue only.
Issued subject to the Company's
By-Laws, Regulations, Bills and Notices.

Wendover
WENDOVER   WENDOVER
TO
GREAT MISSENDEN
Gt MISSENDEN   Gt, MISSENDEN

7d. THIRD   CLASS 7d.

28 AUG

6812

Metropolitan   Railway
NOT TRANSFERABLE
Available on day of issue only.
WENDOVER
WENDOVER   WENDOVER
Series 1   TO   V
HARROW ON THE HILL
HARROW on the HILL HARROW on the HILL
VIA CHALFONT RD
FARE 1/11 THIRD CLASS 1/11

540

540

84.   The LT sign (of paper not enamel) is in contrast to the rural surroundings in this northward view from the early 1960s. The line to the RAF station curved right in the distance and carried freight only, over a distance of 1¾ miles from 1917 until 29th March 1963. (Lens of Sutton coll.)

85.   A 1979 northward view from the footbridge includes the BR replacement sign and the site of the goods yard, which closed on 4th July 1966. Industry now covers the site. The LMR had provided maroon totem signs on a white paper background in September 1961. (B.W.Leslie)

86.　The west elevation was recorded in November 1981. There was no road access to the down side. The bay beyond the main building was used by trains to Halton in the early years. (D.Thompson)

87.　As at Great Missenden, the box was provided with a 30-lever frame, but many of the levers were not used. Closure took place in 1984 and a bypass was later built in the field behind it. Pictures 87 to 91 form a survey undertaken on 20th August 1983. (B.W.Leslie)

88.　Features of the goods yard were recorded in some detail. The north elevation of the shed was entirely of timber construction. (B.W.Leslie)

89.   The hand cranked cranes in most goods sheds were rated at 30 cwt (1½ tons). The small door gave access to the office from where work could be closely observed through the window. (B.W.Leslie)

90.   Larger goods yards were provided with a weighing machine (W.M. on the map) and this building housed the office and instruments. The cast iron bridge for the vehicles was at ground level. A fireplace was standard equipment. (B.W.Leslie)

91.   The hourly DMU to Marylebone is on the canted curve, while a lone passenger waits for a down train. The steps descend from the footbridge onto the cricket field. The bridge has a division to separate passengers from footpath users. (B.W.Leslie)

92.   Temporary fencing separates the platform from the new bypass, over which the footpath is carried on a long span. An up class 165 Turbo is seen on 24th September 1997. (F.Hornby)

STOKE MANDEVILLE

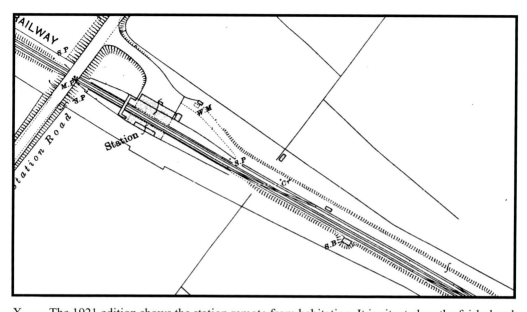

X.   The 1921 edition shows the station remote from habitation. It is situated on the fairly level plain at the foot of the scarp edge of the Chiltern Hills, although the track each side of the station is up at 1 in 117.

93.   An eastward view from the road bridge has the Chilterns in the background and oil lamps on both fences. The population was only 282 in 1901, rising to a mere 1217 by 1961. (Lens of Sutton coll.)

94.   Working to Rickmansworth on 2nd May 1936 is H class 4-4-4T no. 109, which became LNER H2 class no. 6421. The platforms were lengthened at this end in 1960. (H.C.Casserley)

95.   Entering the down platform on the same day is sister locomotive no. 104 (LNER no. 6416). The goods yard is in the left background. The well known Stoke Mandeville Hospital was closer to South Aylesbury Halt on the Princes Risborough line. (H.C.Casserley)

96.   It is 14th January 1962 and a Derby four-car DMU points to the future for the route. With its stylish cats whiskers, it will go only as far as Amersham and slowly on the steep gradients, providing a service of limited appeal. (B.S.Jennings)

97.   BR signs and electric lighting show a degree of modernisation, without detracting from originality. A cover to the footbridge was generous for such a remote location; more surprising is that there was still one in 2005. The sheets had been replaced in 1950 and again in 1987. (Lens of Sutton coll.)

98.   We finish our survey with two photos from 19th November 1981. Little has changed since, except that a modern shelter has arrived on the down platform. (D.Thompson)

99.   The goods yard closed earlier than the others on the route, on 5th July 1965, but like most of its companions, it became a car park. The gradient profile states 1 in 364, but the post on the platform gives 1 in 264. (D.Thompson)

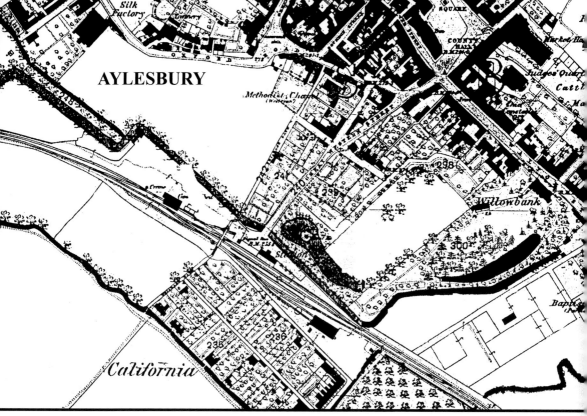

AYLESBURY

XI.   The 1880 edition at 16 ins to one mile has the GWR's single line from Princes Risborough lower right; the parallel track is a siding. The line on the left ran to Verney Junction at that time. Note that Great Western Street ran through orchards to the town centre and that an earlier path is carried over the tracks. The 1863 branch was broad gauge until 1868. The turntable was only 23 ft 9ins long.

100.   The GWR was reluctant to allow Met trains into its station and while the dispute raged, the latter built a temporary wooden platform, accessed from the tracks of this southward view. The lines from the joint station are in the foreground and the sharp reverse curves link with the Amersham line. Aylesbury East box, is in the distance. A 15mph limit was applicable here, but a down newspaper train exceeded this in fog on 23rd December 1904 and an up train collided with the wreckage, resulting in four fatalities. The signal box was replaced by Aylesbury South. (British Railways)

101. The Aylesbury & Buckingham Railway trains used the northern platform (left) and the GWR used the right one until the coming of the Met on 1st January 1894. The GWR thereafter used the one on the extreme right for most services. (Lens of Sutton coll.)

102. The station was further rebuilt in 1925-26. An autotrain bound for Princes Risborough stands near the new building soon afterwards. (Lens of Sutton coll.)

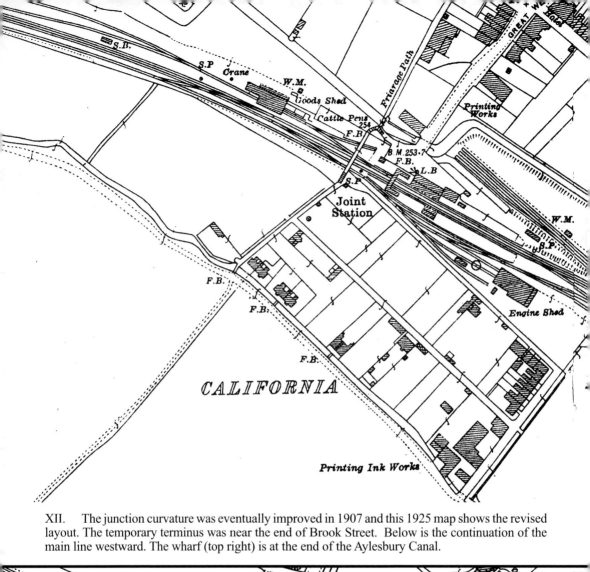

XII.   The junction curvature was eventually improved in 1907 and this 1925 map shows the revised layout. The temporary terminus was near the end of Brook Street. Below is the continuation of the main line westward. The wharf (top right) is at the end of the Aylesbury Canal.

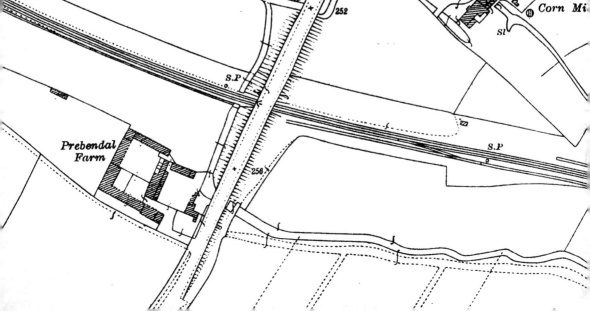

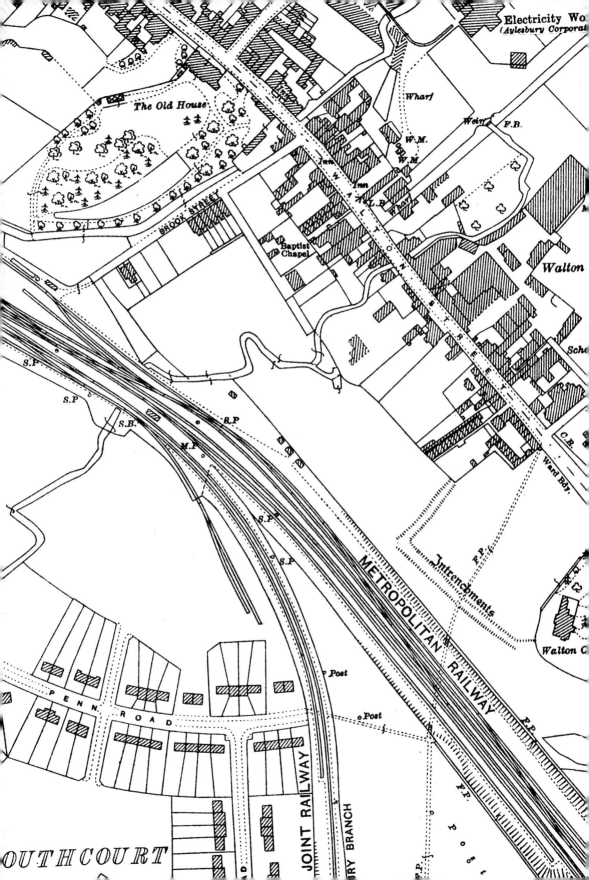

Electricity Wo
(Aylesbury Corporat

The Old House

Wharf

Wein? F.B.

W. M.

W. M.

Inn

Inn

Wharf

Baptist
Chapel

Walton

BROOK STREET

W A L T O N   S T R E E T

Walton

Sch

S.P.

S.P.

S.P.

S.B.

M.P.

C.B.

Ward Bdy.

F.P.

Intrenchments

F.P.

S.P.

S.P.

METROPOLITAN   RAILWAY

Walton C

PENN   ROAD

Post

Post

F.P.

F.P.

OUTHCOURT

JOINT RAILWAY

URY BRANCH

F.P.

Post

103.   Seen in the 1930s is LNER class D10 no. 5436 of 1913 running towards London. Met coaches stand in the bay platform. (Lens of Sutton coll.)

104.   A view north from the up through platform includes cycles on the public footpath, the goods shed and Aylesbury North signal box, which closed in 1967. Freight service ceased on 2nd December 1974. (Lens of Sutton coll.)

105.   The scene in poor light on 20th July 1951 includes class N5 0-6-2T no. 69302 (left) bound for Princes Risborough and class L1 2-6-4T no. 67720, with a Baker Street train. Both engines were ex-LNER. Part of the end wall of the engine shed was later removed to allow one track to be extended. (T.J.Edgington)

106.   A carriage siding is below the camera as class L1 no. 67753 departs in perfect light at 1.09pm on 2nd November 1953. Its shed code plate shows 34E, which is Neasden. (N.W.Sprinks)

107.   The bay platform on the north side of the station was added in 1926. There was a cattle dock to the north of it. The bay was numbered 1; freight is passing through No.2 on 3rd September 1961. (J.C.Gillham)

3rd Cl   M&GC
SERVICES LEAVE TICKET.
Issued subject to the Bye-Laws, Regulations and
Conditions of theCommittee and to the Special
Conditions relating to Cheap Tickets
Available for three Days

AYLESBURY to
CALVERT
Via Quainton Road
Not Transferable

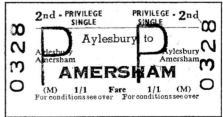

2nd · PRIVILEGE   PRIVILEGE · 2nd
            SINGLE   SINGLE
P   Aylesbury to   P
Aylesbury   Aylesbury
Amersham   Amersham
AMERSHAM
(M)   1/1   Fare   1/1   (M)
For conditions see over   For conditions see over

108.   Approaching platform 3 on the same day is ex-LNER class B1 4-6-0 no. 61112 with a long-distance train from Marylebone. The Princes Risborough line is on the right. (J.C.Gillham)

109.   Platform 4 is examined in this trio of 1961 photos. Met trains ceased to run to Aylesbury on 11th September of that year and the engine shed was not used after 1963. (J.C.Gillham)

110.   Class 5 4-6-0 no. 45217 takes water near the public footbridge during its stop at platform 3, while working the 12.40pm Marylebone to Nottingham service on 1st November 1961. (B.S.Jennings)

111.   Running into platform 2 on 9th June 1962 is class B1 no. 61186 with the 1.30pm from Nottingham Victoria. The massive goods shed is in the background. (B.S.Jennings)

Other views of this station can be found in our
Branch Lines to Princes Risborough.
Aylesbury High Street station appears in our
Watford to Leighton Buzzard album.

112.   The first engine shed had a single broad gauge track and a lean-to extension for another line followed in 1868. It was replaced by this structure in about 1900. The first tank drawings were dated 1878, but this one was built later. (Lens of Sutton coll.)

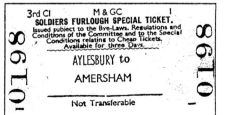

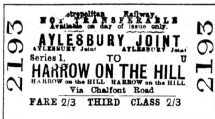

113. Still standing in 1967, this sign hints at the complex administration of this station; its engine shed and signal boxes were also subject to similar problems. The suffix "Town" was used from 1950 until 1963 and also at other times unofficially. LT civil engineers trains were recorded here as late as October 1966. (H.C.Casserley)

114. The bay platform and associated sidings were taken out of use in November 1990, ten years after this photograph was taken. Carriage accommodation south of the station was increased in the early 1990s, with three on the down side and four on the up. (T.Heavyside)

115.   A DMU leaves for Amersham at 14.09 on 28th September 1980, the assorted livery being a feature of the period. The signal box closed on 3rd December 1990. (T.Heavyside)

116.   Seen in 1989, the classic buffet would have a limited life. It was replaced by a small bar in the entrance area. The GWR logo had been added in the 1970s. (P.G.Barnes)

117.   This is the scene on 30th May 1991 as modernisation and repair work was in progress. The DMU is standing alongside the new signalling centre, which controlled the northern part of the route from December 1990. (F.Hornby)

118. A western panorama from the bridge in the background of picture 111 features the DMU servicing depot, completed in 1991 for the new fleet of Turbos. Until that time, units ran to Bletchley via Verney Junction for maintenance. (D.B.Clayton)

119.   As seen in the previous photo, Chiltern Railways retain a few of the early BR DMUs. This railcar was in use for sandite application, while another was refurbished for passenger use to Princes Risborough. This and the next view date from 18th April 2005. (V.Mitchell)

120.   The town needed enlarged facilities, as it grew from 9243 folk in 1901 to 31,030 in 1961. This was the result of the LNER's effort, although the Met made a contribution to the cost. It serves as an appropriate approach to a train service greatly enhanced in recent years. (V.Mitchell)

MP Middleton Press

Easebourne Lane, Midhurst, West Sussex. GU29 9AZ Tel:01730 813169

EVOLVING THE ULTIMATE RAIL ENCYCLOPEDIA

www.middletonpress.co.uk email:info@middletonpress.co.uk

A-0 906520 B-1 873793 C-1 901706 D-1 904474

OOP Out of Print at time of printing - Please check current availability **BROCHURE AVAILABLE SHOWING NEW TITLES**